The Canadian Shield

Tina Schwartzenberger

Weigl

CALGARY
www.weigl.ca

Published by Weigl Educational Publishers Limited
6325 – 10 Street SE
Calgary, Alberta, Canada
T2H 2Z9

Web site: www.weigl.ca

Library and Archives Canada Cataloguing in Publication

Schwartzenberger, Tina
        The Canadian Shield / Tina Schwartzenberger.
(Canadian geographic regions)
Includes index.
ISBN 1-55388-141-9 (bound).--1-55388-148-6 (pbk.)
        1. Canadian Shield--Geography--Textbooks. I. Title. II. Series.
FC58.S39 2005   917.14   C2005-904572-8

Printed in the United States of America
1 2 3 4 5 6 7 8 9 0   09 08 07 06 05

CREDITS: Every reasonable effort has been made to trace ownership and to obtain permission to
reprint copyright material. The publishers would be pleased to have any errors or omissions brought
to their attention so that they may be corrected in subsequent printings.

COVER: Aurora borealis are also known as northern lights. They occur frequently above 60° north
latitude, which contains much of the Canadian Shield.

Cover: Wayne R. Bilenduke/Photographer's Choice/Getty Images (front); Norbert Rosing/National
Geographic/Getty Images (back); **Getty Images:** pages 3 (Wayne R. Bilenduke/Photographer's Choice),
4L (Steve Bly/The Image Bank), 4ML (Paul Nicklen/National Geographic), 4MR (Philip & Karen
Smith/Stone), 4R (Francesca York/Dorling Kindersley), 5L (Raymond K. Gehman/National
Geographic), 5M (John Dunn/National Geographic), 5R (Ed Simpson/Stone), 6 (Altrendo
nature/Altrendo), 7L (Photodisc Collection/Photodisc Blue), 7R (Raymond Gehman/National
Geographic), 11 (Hans Strand/The Image Bank), 13L (Grant Dixon/Lonely Planet Images), 13R (S.
Lowry/Univ Ulster/Stone), 14 (Hulton Archive), 15 (Norbert Rosing/National Geographic), 16 (Time
Life Pictures), 17 (Hulton Archive), 18 (John Dunn/National Geographic), 19 (Eastcott Momatiuk/The
Image Bank), 20 (Jeremy Hoare/Life File/Photodisc Green), 21 (Raymond Gehman/National
Geographic), 22 (Paul Nicklen/National Geographic), 23 (Grant Dixon/Lonely Planet Images), 24
(Grant Dixon/Lonely Planet Images), 25 (Norbert Rosing/National Geographic), 28 (David R.
Frazier/Stone), 29 (Wayne R. Bilenduke/Stone), 30 (George F. Herben/National Geographic), 31
(Lester Lefkowitz/The Image Bank), 32 (Alexandra Grablewski/Botanica), 33 (Michael Orton/Stone),
34 (PhotoLink/Photodisc Green), 35 (Peter Essick/Aurora), 36 (Eastcott Momatiuk/The Image Bank),
37 (Jim Merli/Visuals Unlimited), 38 (Peter Essick/Aurora), 40 (Raymond Gehman/National
Geographic), 41 (Astromujoff/The Image Bank), 42 (Nancy Simmerman/Stone), 43TL (Getty
Images/Taxi), 43TR (Nicholas Veasey/Photographer's Choice), 43ML (Tom Schierlitz/The Image
Bank), 43MR (Bill Greenblatt/Liaison), 43BL (Maria Stenzel/National Geographic), 43BR (Bryce Flynn
Photography Inc/Taxi), 44L (Stockdisc/Stockdisc Classic), 44M (Ryan McVay/Photodisc Green), 44R
(C Squared Studios/Photodisc Green), 45L (Tom Schierlitz/The Image Bank), 45R
(Stockdisc/Stockdisc Classic).

Copy Editors
Frances Purslow
Janice L. Redlin
Arlene Worsley

Designer
Terry Paulhus

Layout
Kathryn Livingstone
Gregg Muller

Photo Researchers
Annalise Bekkering
Jennifer Hurtig

We acknowledge the financial
support of the Government of
Canada through the Book
Publishing Industry Development
Program (BPIDP) for our
publishing activities.

CONTENTS

The Regions of Canada

Canada is the second largest country on Earth. It occupies an enormous area of land on the North American continent. Studying geography helps draw attention to the seven diverse Canadian regions, including their land, climate, vegetation, and wildlife. Learning about geography also helps in understanding the people in each region, their history, and their culture. The word "geography" comes from Greek and means "earth description."

THE APPALACHIAN	THE CANADIAN SHIELD	THE CORDILLERA	THE GREAT LAKES
The Appalachian region is named for the Appalachian mountain range that extends from the United States into eastern Canada. This diverse region contains highlands, lowlands, plateaus, hills, coastal areas, lakes, and rivers.	By far the largest of Canada's geographic regions, the Canadian Shield occupies almost half of the total area of Canada. It is centred around the Hudson Bay. The Canadian Shield is characterized by rocky, poor soil and cold temperatures.	The Cordillera region comprises a series of mountain belts in western Canada. It includes three significant mountain ranges—the Rocky Mountains, Coast Mountains, and Columbia Mountains.	The Great Lakes region is home to five lakes—Lake Superior, Lake Huron, Lake Ontario, Lake Michigan, and Lake Erie. Together, they make up the largest freshwater region in the world.

Canada is home to a variety of landforms. The country hosts sweeping Arctic **tundra**, fertile lowlands, rolling plains, majestic mountains, and vast forests. Each region has a wide range of plants, animals, natural resources, industries, and people.

THE INTERIOR PLAINS	THE NORTH	THE ST. LAWRENCE LOWLANDS
The rolling, low-lying landscape of the Interior Plains is the primary centre for agriculture in Canada. The Interior Plains region lies between the Cordillera and the Canadian Shield.	Much of the North region is composed of thousands of islands north of the Canadian mainland. Distinctive landforms in the region include Arctic lowlands and polar deserts. Glacier mountains are also a recognizable feature in the North.	The St. Lawrence Lowlands region is located on fertile soil surrounding the St. Lawrence River. The region contains a waterway system linking Canada and the United States to the Atlantic Ocean.

Welcome to the Canadian Shield

Spanning almost half of Canada, the Canadian Shield is the country's largest geographic region. This enormous area covers most of Quebec, Ontario, and Newfoundland, northern Manitoba and Saskatchewan, and parts of Alberta, the Northwest Territories, and Nunavut. The Shield also extends into Minnesota, Wisconsin, Michigan, and New York in the United States.

> " The Canadian Shield is the largest region in Canada, spreading across six provinces and two territories. "

Viewing the Canadian Shield from above, its shape resembles a horseshoe, with Hudson Bay acting as its centre. Rocky hills, rolling uplands, vast forests, and tundra dot the Shield's landscape. It neighbours other regions, including the Interior Plains, the North, and the Appalachian. It also extends into the United States. In this way, the Shield forms a rough semi-circle.

The Canadian Shield is covered with countless rivers and lakes. These range in size from small ponds to large lakes such as Lake Athabasca.

Other Kinds of Value

The Canadian Shield has little fertile land that is suitable for agriculture. It contains ample forests, mineral resources, and water. The numerous rivers and lakes in the Shield provide hydroelectricity to many Canadians. Although the Canadian Shield contains many rocks, only 10 percent are exposed. Most rocks are hidden under thin soil, dense bush, or **muskeg**.

Black bears are found throughout the Canadian Shield region. The diet of the black bear is about 95 percent vegetation and about 5 percent insects, mammals, and birds.

Trees such as birch can grow as far north as the northern edge of the Canadian Shield.

QUICK FACTS

- Plateaus dominate the eastern part of the Canadian Shield.

- Belts of hills lie between uplands and plateaus across the Shield.

- Granite and gneiss are the most common rocks on the Canadian Shield.

Map of Canadian Geographic Regions

This map of Canada shows the seven geographic regions that make up the country. The regions are divided by their topography, from towering mountains to river valleys, and from Arctic tundra to rolling prairies. Canadian geographic regions are some of the most diverse anywhere in the world.

Studying a map of Canada's geographic regions helps develop an understanding of them, and about the nation as a whole.

LEGEND

- The Appalachian
- The Canadian Shield
- The Cordillera
- The Great Lakes
- The Interior Plains
- The North
- The St. Lawrence Lowlands

0   500 Kilometres

Latitude and Longitude

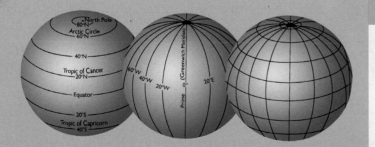

Longitude measures the distance from a spot on the map to an imaginary line called the prime meridian that runs around the globe from the North Pole to the South Pole.

Latitude measures the distance from a spot on the map to an imaginary line called the equator that runs around the middle of the globe.

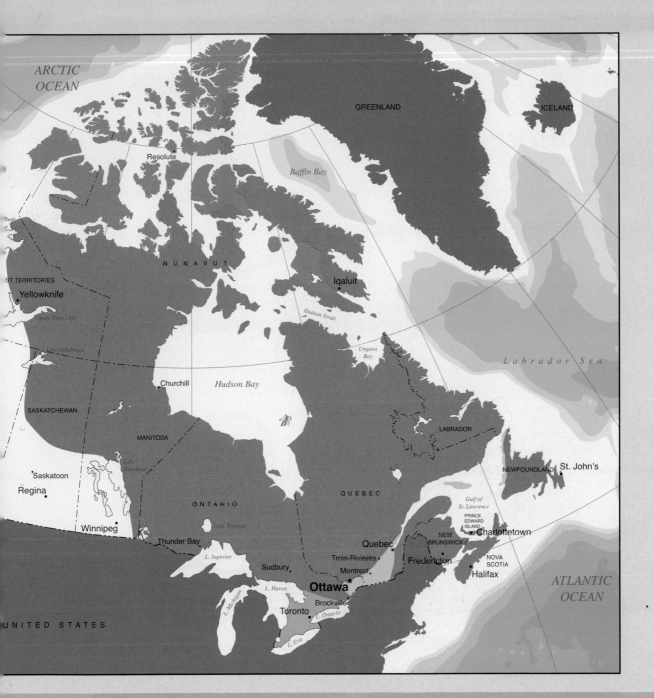

The Map Scale

A map scale is a type of formula. The scale helps determine how to calculate distances between places on a map.

0   500 Kilometres

The Compass Rose

North is indicated on the map by the compass rose. As well, the cardinal directions—north, south, east, and west—and the intermediate directions—northeast, southeast, northwest, southwest—are shown.

Forming the Earth

Geographers and other scientists study geographic regions, climate, animals, and vegetation. Scientists have learned that many regions on different continents have similar characteristics.

The Story of Pangaea

The reason Earth has similar regions in different countries is that the world was once made up of one continent, or landmass. In 1912, Alfred Wegener, a German geologist and meteorologist, called this supercontinent Pangaea. He proposed the theory that Pangaea covered nearly half of Earth's surface and was surrounded by an ocean called Panthalassa. Between 245 and 208 million years ago, Pangaea began to split. Pieces of the landmass moved apart forming the seven continents—Africa, Antarctica, Asia, Australia, Europe, North America, and South America.

PERMIAN
225 million years ago

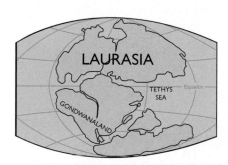

TRIASSIC
200 million years ago

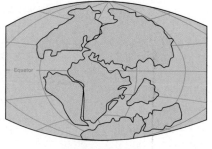

JURASSIC
135 million years ago

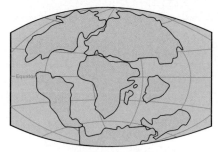

CRETACEOUS
65 million years ago

Ancient rocks expose a long history of mountain building, and erosion in the region.

Sharing with the Shield

Other continents have regions similar to the Canadian Shield. The Baltic, or Fennoscandian, Shield spreads over most of Finland, Sweden, and eastern Norway. The African Shield covers western Saudi Arabia and the eastern half of Madagascar, as well as half of of Africa.

Similar to the Canadian Shield, these continental shields contain rocks that are millions of years old. While each shield shares similar types of soil, plants, and animals, the Canadian Shield is the only continental shield in the world that has been affected by glaciers. During the last **Ice Age**, glaciers scraped across the surface of the region, further eroding the land.

Naming the Shield

In 1883, Austrian geologist Eduard Suess used the word "shield" to describe the region. He thought it looked like a warrior's shield lying flat on the ground.

QUICK FACTS

- The northern part of Pangaea was called Laurasia. The southern part was called Gondwanaland.

- *Pangaea* is a Greek word that means "all Earth."

- Earth's crust is broken into many pieces called plates. The plates are in very slow, constant motion and move 1.3 to 10 centimetres each year.

- Scientists have found fossils of tropical plants and animals in North America. The fossils tell scientists that North America was once located farther south than its present location.

Millions of Years Ago

The Canadian Shield began forming about 3 billion years ago as part of Earth's crust, or surface layer. This period of time is called the Precambrian era, which is why the Canadian Shield is sometimes called the Precambrian Shield. The formation of North America is revealed through the rocks of the Canadian Shield, which make up 85 percent of Earth's history.

Pressure deep inside Earth folded and crumpled the **metamorphic rocks** of the Canadian Shield, forming mountains. Intense heat and pressure also changed rocks. **Igneous** rocks became metamorphic rocks. The high temperatures and extreme pressure enabled **minerals** to form. Today, the Canadian Shield is incredibly rich in mineral resources.

Since the mountains formed, billions of years of **erosion** have worn them down. The Shield represents the remnants of the mountains' core. It forms the foundation of the North American continent.

The Glacial Erosion on the Canadian Shield Surface

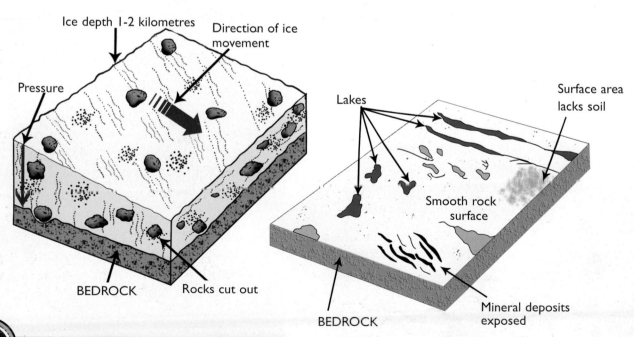

Ice depth 1-2 kilometres

Direction of ice movement

Pressure

BEDROCK

Rocks cut out

Lakes

Surface area lacks soil

Smooth rock surface

Mineral deposits exposed

BEDROCK

Glaciers Carve the Land

As the temperature grew colder, glaciers spread across North America. This period of time is called an ice age. Four ice ages, each lasting about 100,000 years, brought ice sheets that wore down the mountains that once covered the Canadian Shield.

With warm temperatures, glacial movement eroded the mountains even further, leaving a very thin layer of soil on top of **bedrock**. The roots of the mountains were exposed and formed the continent's surface.

Glacial movement gouged deep pits and valleys in the land, forming depressions. Lakes and rivers were created when the water from melting glaciers rushed into these depressions.

The Penny Ice Cap in Auyuittuq National Park is thought to be the source of ice that covered Canada during the last Ice Age.

WHAT HAPPENED DURING THE PRECAMBRIAN ERA?

The Precambrian era is the longest period in Earth's history. It is also the oldest period in Earth's history that can be studied today. For over 3.5 billion years, Earth's atmosphere and oceans formed from gases that had escaped Earth's hot interior during volcanic eruptions. Nitrogen gas, carbon dioxide, and water vapour combined to form the atmosphere. As Earth's temperature cooled, water vapour condensed, falling to the ground as precipitation.

Life on Earth also began during the Precambrian era. Scientists have found **fossils**, such as **prokaryotes**, in sedimentary rock. Prokaryotes appeared between 3.8 billion and 3.5 billion years ago. These simple organisms were anaerobic, meaning they did not require oxygen. In Earth's early days, oxygen barely existed in the atmosphere.

The First Inhabitants

Although few people live on the Canadian Shield today, some people have lived in the region for as long as anyone can remember. Some scientists believe that the first people to live on the Canadian Shield were Palaeoindians, who have come to be known as Shield Archaic people. Their means of survival depended on hunting big-game animals, such as mammoths, big-horned bison, and possibly mastodons.

> " Some scientists believe that the first people to live on the Canadian Shield were Palaeoindians, who have come to be known as Shield Archaic people. "

Ancient Evidence

In the early 1960s, evidence of Shield Archaic people on the Canadian Shield was discovered near the Acasta River, about 130 kilometres southeast of Great Bear Lake in the Northwest Territories. Thirty years later, some of the world's oldest known rocks were discovered at this same site.

People from the ice ages adapted to life in the boreal forest of the Canadian Shield. They began drifting south and east, providing the cultural roots for today's **Algonquian** peoples.

The wigwam was an easily moved dwelling for nomadic Algonquian tribes.

The Inuit Arrive

The earliest Inuit arrived in North America about 4,000 years ago. They adapted to life along the northern edge of the **boreal forest**.

Athapaskan, or Dene, peoples and Algonquians lived in the forested parts of the Canadian Shield. The Algonquians include Naskapi, Ojibwa, Cree, Ottawa, **Algonquin**, and Montagnais, or Innu. Family groups spread out across the region.

Dome-shaped igloos, which were once Inuit dwellings, are built spirally from within.

Early Life on the Shield

Small groups lived together. Large groups could not survive because access to food was limited. Groups of hunters used spears, lances, bows and arrows, traps, and snares. They hunted caribou, moose, beaver, and bear for food. The Cree found geese a valuable food source, catching and freezing them for later use. Fish could be caught in the region's many rivers and lakes.

The original inhabitants of the Canadian Shield were nomadic. They travelled around the region, often moving with the seasons. Dogs hauled people's belongings from campsite to campsite. These peoples lived in wigwams, which are dwellings built from caribou or moose hides stretched across poles.

WHO LIVES ON THE CANADIAN SHIELD?

Eight percent of Canada's population lives on the Canadian Shield. Today, more than 2 million people in Quebec and Ontario live in the region. First Nation Peoples who presently live on the Canadian Shield live near mining or forestry towns.

The Canadian Shield has many small and medium-sized communities. Most communities range from 200 to more than 1,000 residents. The two largest communities on the Canadian Shield are Sudbury, Ontario, with a population of 155,900, and Chicoutimi, Quebec, with a population of just over 1 million. Residents in all communities on the Shield come from a variety of ethnic backgrounds.

Exploration and the Fur Trade

The first Europeans to see the Canadian Shield were the **Norse**. In 986 AD, a Norseman named Biarni Heriulfson was sailing the Atlantic Ocean. His ship was blown off course onto the east coast of Newfoundland. Between 1000 and 1350, Europeans from Greenland and Iceland made multiple landings on the shores of northern Canada. Some believe that Sir Henry Sinclair, Earl of Orkney, who was born in Scotland, landed on Baffin Island in 1398. In 1497, John Cabot claimed Newfoundland for King Henry VII of Great Britain.

Fur Trade Spurs Exploration

The fur trade was vital to Canada's development. Furs from animals such as beaver were in high demand in Europe. Europeans in Canada traded with First Nations Peoples for furs. The employees of the two biggest fur trade companies—the Hudson's Bay Company and the North West Company—were largely responsible for exploring the Canadian Shield region.

John Cabot and his three sons were the first British citizens to embark on a journey for unknown lands to the west.

In 1771, Samuel Hearne, an employee of the Hudson's Bay Company, was one of the first Europeans to reach the Canadian Shield. He, along with other explorers who followed him, hoped to find the **Northwest Passage**. Many people in Europe believed that a water route travelled through Canada's Arctic to the riches of Asia.

Peter Pond, an American explorer who worked for the North West Company, mapped the Great Slave Lake region in the Northwest Territories between 1768 and 1788. In 1789, Sir Alexander Mackenzie, a Scottish explorer also working for the North West Company, became the first European to canoe to the Arctic Ocean. The river he travelled was named the Mackenzie River in his honour.

First Settlements

Few Europeans permanently settled on the Canadian Shield. They established relationships with the First Nations Peoples living in the region. In the twentieth century, people continued to explore the Canadian Shield region. Today, some regions of the Canadian Shield remain unexplored.

WHO WAS SAMUEL HEARNE?

Samuel Hearne was born in London, Great Britain, in 1745. He joined the Hudson's Bay Company in 1766. Hearne was chosen to search for a western passage across "The Barren Lands," or the Canadian Shield. He became the first European to cross these barren lands.

Hearne twice attempted to find the Northwest Passage. Both attempts failed. On December 7, 1770, he left Prince of Wales Fort with Matonabbee, a prestigious Chipewyan leader. Hearne and Matonabbee walked across the Shield, following migration patterns of caribou for 19 months.

Hearne wrote about his expedition, offering a description of his sufferings in the barren land, and a detailed description of Matonabbee and his people. Hearne's greatest accomplishment was learning how to survive in the cold wilderness. He gained this knowledge from the First Nation Peoples.

Tales from the Canadian Shield

A DENE STORY: CREATION OF SEASONS

First Nations tales from the Canadian Shield often describe how Earth and its creatures were born. This story explains how Dene hunters freed spring and summer from bears.

The first people of Earth had to endure winter for the entire 12 months of the year. Most of the land was covered by large, moving layers of ice and deep snow. No trees, bushes, or flowers could survive in the harsh cold. The lakes and rivers were frozen, so no water flowed.

One day the first people came upon a bear who had a sack around his neck. The hunters asked the bear what was in the sack. The bear growled a reply that he had a sack filled with the abundance of summer's warmth and light. The hunters wanted the sack and offered to trade, but the bear would not part with his sack. The hunters begged the bear, but still he refused to give up his sack.

The hunters' chief then planned a great feast to lure the bear so they could steal his sack. The bear arrived in the evening for the feast of moose and caribou, but he did not have the sack around his neck.

After the feast, the chief sent hunters to follow the bear home and steal the sack. They came to a large cave and saw the sack inside, with two bears guarding it. A fierce fight killed three of the hunters and mortally wounded the fourth, but before he died, the fourth hunter grabbed the sack and unleashed the warmth and light. Instantly, the air became warm, and the sky filled with bright sunlight. The snow melted into rivers and lakes. The hills and valleys were covered with trees, flowers, and bushes. Every year since, summer has come to the Dene.

HOW THE MOUSE SAVED THE SUN

First Nations Peoples in the Pukaskwa area of Ontario tell a story about how darkness lingered because the Sun was trapped in a snare. The Anishnaba people asked a mouse to set the Sun free.

There was once an Anishnabe village full of Anishnaba people. One day, an Anishnaba person went out on the land to set some snares.

The next day, it was time for daylight, but no daylight came. The Anishnabe village people knew something was wrong because the Sun did not come up. The Anishnabe person who had set snares the day before said, "I will go and look for my snares in the dark. Maybe I got something on my snares."

When he came to one of his snares, he saw that he had caught the Sun in his snare! The Sun was too hot to set free, so the Anishnabe went back to the village.

"What happened," he said to them, "is that I caught the Sun in my snare. That is why the Sun cannot come up." They called a meeting, and everyone, including the animals and birds, was asked to come. They were told that someone had to free the Sun.

One mouse, which was the biggest animal, was asked if he was willing to free the Sun.

"Okay," said the big mouse, "I will go and free the Sun." So, he went. He came to the snare where the Sun was caught. The mouse started to chew the snare wire. Even though he was burning, he did not give up. The mouse kept on chewing snare wire until the Sun was free.

Finally, the Sun was free, and it was daylight again. The tiny mouse we see today is the mouse that freed the Sun from the snare. He was once a big mouse. His small size shows how much he burned before he was able to free the Sun. Now the mouse is the smallest animal.

Forests and Water

The Canadian Shield is not a barren landscape. It has a largely rocky surface, with additional features such as forests, rivers, lakes, hills, valleys, and marshes. Rivers in the region flow south into the Gulf of St. Lawrence or east into the Atlantic Ocean. Spruce forests dominate the interior of the region. Many inlets provide protected areas for people to settle along the coastline.

> **The Canadian Shield has a largely rocky surface, with additional features such as forests, rivers, lakes, hills, valleys, and marshes.**

Boreal Forest

The boreal forest on the Canadian Shield separates the Arctic tundra from the southern deciduous forests. The boreal forest is made up of **coniferous** trees, such as pines, cedars, black and white spruce, and fir. Birch and aspen trees are also part of the boreal forest. The boreal forest has long, cold winters and short, hot, wet summers. The region receives about 70 centimetres of precipitation each year. More than half of the precipitation is in the form of rain. Snow covers the ground for 5 months each year.

Rivers and Lakes

The Canadian Shield contains a large quantity of water. Glacial movement from the ice ages left deep depressions in the land. These depressions filled with melted glacier water, forming rivers and lakes.

Most of Canada's larger lakes are found on the Canadian Shield. Great Bear Lake, Great Slave Lake, Lake Athabasca, and Lake Winnipeg are all found within this region. The region also borders some of the Great Lakes.

Climate in the boreal forests of the Canadian Shield is influenced by cold air masses from Hudson Bay.

Muskeg

Most of the Canadian Shield lies near sea level. Water in these low-lying areas rests in wetlands called muskeg. These wetlands also include marshes and **bogs**. Drainage is generally poor throughout the Canadian Shield.

Often, plants do not grow well under pine trees. Pine needles are very acidic, and they make the soil under the trees too acidic for many plants to survive.

Muskeg is covered with mosses, grasses, and sometimes even trees. It consists of dead plants, including peat and sphagnum moss.

The ground in these wetlands is not firm. Muskeg is very **porous** and cannot support weight. This proved to be a challenge when the Canadian Pacific Railway was constructed in the nineteenth century.

QUICK FACTS

> The boreal forest takes its name from Boreas, the Greek god of the north wind.

> The granite rock found beneath the Canadian Shield's lakes does not dissolve in water. There is little vegetation in the water, so the lake water is very clear.

> Water covers more than one quarter of the Canadian Shield's surface.

A contractor named Joseph Whitehead was building a section of railway near present-day Kenora, Ontario. He spent $80,000 to pour 198,000 square metres of gravel into a swamp in order to build a strong base on which to build the railway track. Whitehead went bankrupt and was unable to complete construction. The Canadian government assumed responsibility for this part of the Canadian Pacific Railway.

Landforms

The Canadian Shield region has hills, plateaus, valleys, and the remnants of mountains. The area extending from northwestern Quebec through northern Ontario, Manitoba, Saskatchewan, and parts of Nunavut and the Northwest Territories is classified as upland. The region is mainly upland because it is elevated above the Hudson Bay lowland and Interior Plains region that surround it.

Plateaus of the Shield

The eastern part of the Canadian Shield consists of mostly plateaus. Near the coasts, the average elevation of the land is 180 to 365 metres above sea level. From central Newfoundland to Quebec, the elevation is 900 metres. Valleys cutting into higher terrain create a **relief** of 150 to 300 metres.

Highlands

The eastern and southeastern portion of the Canadian Shield, including northern Newfoundland and parts of Baffin Island, is classified as highland. This mountainous land stands 800 to 1,500 metres above sea level. Rolling plateaus are cut by glacial troughs. The coastline is dotted with **fjords**.

Some small streams plunge hundreds of metres over the edge of a fjord, creating high waterfalls.

The Thousand Islands

Across the St. Lawrence River, from eastern Ontario into New York's Adirondack Mountains, the Canadian Shield rises out of the water. This 80-kilometre projection takes the form of the Thousand Islands. More than 1,000 rocky, wooded islands mark Lake Ontario between Kingston and Brockville. Some islands measure many square kilometres, while others are mere projections of rock.

Athabasca Sand Dunes

An **anomaly** in this region is the Athabasca sand dunes. The sand dunes along the south side of Lake Athabasca, located in northern Alberta and Saskatchewan, are the longest in Canada. Most sand dunes are found in dry, desert-like areas, but the Athabasca sand dunes border 7,850 square kilometres of water. Some visitors have seen trees emerging from the shifting sand of the dunes. The trees were buried by the sand long ago, and wind has exposed them over time.

There are many fjords and glacier-laden mountains on Baffin Island. Peaks reach up to 2,000 metres in height.

QUICK FACTS

- Most of the Canadian Shield's upland region ranges from 300 to 500 metres above sea level.

- Mount Caubvick, the highest point on Newfoundland, is 1,652 metres. It is located in the Torngat Mountains.

- The Canadian Shield was the first part of North America to be permanently elevated above sea level.

Long Winters, Short Summers

The Canadian Shield's climate varies throughout the region. The climate ranges from arctic to subarctic. Arctic climate has year-round cold temperatures that prevent trees from growing. Subarctic climate features cold winter temperatures, but the temperature warms enough in summer to allow some tree growth.

In the northern part of the Canadian Shield, winters are long and cold, while summers are short and warm. In the southern part of the region, summers are cool and wet, while fog and heavy snowfalls occur during winter. The eastern part of the Canadian Shield has milder winter temperatures, which average -1° Celsius. Winter temperatures average -20° Celsius on the western edge of the Canadian Shield. Throughout the region, summer temperatures average 13° Celsius.

During summer, wind on the Canadian Shield blows from the south. In the fall, the Arctic air mass moves south of the tree line, shifting the warmer southern air mass as it moves. This air movement brings storms to the Canadian Shield region.

Auyuittuq National Park Reserve in Nunavut is a harsh land of barren tundra, jagged mountain peaks, deep fjords, and ice.

In January and February, the Hudson Bay becomes covered with ice.
This brings very cold temperatures to the Canadian Shield.

Gale-force winds occur in September and October, while November and December receive heavy snowfall. By January, snowstorms are less frequent, but the air is bitterly cold.

Snow and More Snow

Deep in the boreal forest, the effects of wind are minimal. Soil below the snow is usually warmer and more moist than the air above the snow. Heat and moisture flow upward to the upper layers of cooler, drier snow. Water molecules rise until they condense and refreeze on colder snow above. Over winter, the lower layers of snow get smaller and weaker. The upper layers grow thicker and stronger. Eventually, the snow is reduced to tiny balls of ice that look and feel like sugar. This is called corn snow.

Sun and Rain

The Canadian Shield's sunniest season, summer, is also its rainiest. August is the rainiest month. Rain often falls 1 out of every 3 days. The western part of the Canadian Shield receives about 400 millimetres of precipitation each year. Some areas of Newfoundland receive as much as 1,600 millimetres of precipitation. This area receives more precipitation because it is close to the Atlantic Ocean.

QUICK FACTS

- Hudson Bay is frozen from late December until late June. The ice melts during summer, but the surface water temperature remains close to freezing.

- Snow covers the ground for 5 months each year. The snow's temperature rarely falls below -7° Celsius. Snow provides an insulating blanket for the animals living in the Canadian Shield region.

- The ice on Great Slave Lake can be 1 metre thick in January. A 20,000 kilogram bulldozer can sit on the lake ice.

Charting the Climate

A region's climate can indicate what it is like to live there. Temperature, snowfall, and even growing seasons are all part of climate.

Information is collected when studying a region's climate. The maps and charts on these pages help describe this information in a visual way.

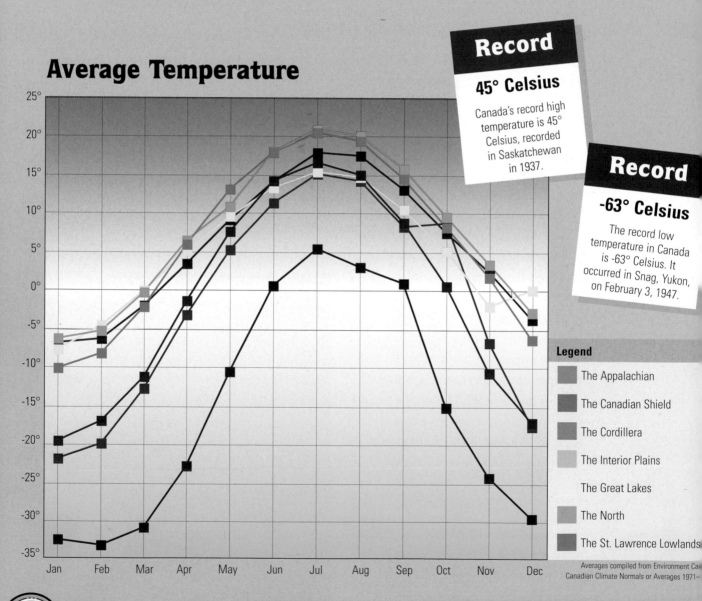

Average Temperature

Record

45° Celsius

Canada's record high temperature is 45° Celsius, recorded in Saskatchewan in 1937.

Record

-63° Celsius

The record low temperature in Canada is -63° Celsius. It occurred in Snag, Yukon, on February 3, 1947.

Legend

- The Appalachian
- The Canadian Shield
- The Cordillera
- The Interior Plains
- The Great Lakes
- The North
- The St. Lawrence Lowlands

Averages compiled from Environment Ca
Canadian Climate Normals or Averages 1971–

Average Snowfall

Legend

- over 400 cm
- 300 - 400 cm
- 200 - 300 cm
- 100 - 200 cm
- under 100 cm

Source: Canadian Oxford World Atlas, 4th Edition, 1998

Record

118.1 cm

The record 1-day snowfall, on January 17, 1974, was 118.1 centimetres at Lakelse Lake, British Columbia.

Growing Season

Legend

Average number of days with a median temperature over 5° C

- under 60
- 60 - 100
- 100 - 140
- 140 - 180
- 180 - 220
- 220 - 260
- over 260

Source: Canadian Oxford World Atlas, 4th Edition, 1998

Raging Fires

Many trees cover the Canadian Shield. Hot, dry summers account for the forest fires that are frequent in this region. With the region so sparsely populated, people seldom lose their lives in these fires. Canada's deadliest forest fire occurred on the Canadian Shield in 1916, when more than 200 people died in the Matheson, Ontario, fire.

Dry Summer Leading to Disaster

Matheson is a small town on the Canadian Shield. In the summer of 1916, settlers were clearing the land of trees. The settlers cut down trees for building materials and burned unwanted timber. Sometimes the settlers lost control of the burning, causing fires to occur. It was a very dry summer, with no rain for weeks. By July 27, many of the timber fires had grown dangerous.

On July 29, 1916, high winds fanned the flames and created one large fire, extending 64 kilometres. The fire burned in an easterly direction at a rate of 40 to 60 kilometres per hour.

Large forest fires still occur in Canadian forests, but modern detection and firefighting techniques decrease their threat.

Towns Destroyed

In just one day, the fire destroyed the settlements of Iroquois Falls, Porquis Junction, Kelso, Nushka, Matheson, and Ramore. In total, the fire destroyed forty-nine townships.

In 1916, fire-fighting techniques were far less sophisticated than they are today. Efforts to fight or control the fire had little effect. The fire was finally brought under control in early August when rain began falling. About 5,000 hectares of forest were destroyed. The exact number of lives lost is unknown, but the estimate of 223 remains on record.

Factors such as fire, climate, and soil have played a major role in shaping Canada's forests.

HOW DID THE FIRE AFFECT THE REGION?

The Matheson fire had a positive result because it showed the need for organized efforts to fight forest fires. In December 1916, a Forest Protection Branch was added to the Department of Lands, Forests, and Mines. In 1917, the Ontario legislature passed the Forest Fires Prevention Act. This act is the basis of Ontario's forest protection laws today. The act also aims to prevent another terrible tragedy, such as the Matheson fire, from occurring again.

Despite the tragedy, forest fires are an important natural event in the Canadian Shield region. Lightning has caused most forest fires in the region since the first trees began growing after the glaciers melted. Each square kilometre of forest has probably been burned at least 40 times. Fire-scarred trees and charred stumps and branches litter the forests. Still, fire sustains the forest.

Without fire, forests would be unproductive. Fire prunes aging trees and breathes new life into forests. Fire releases nutrients stored in the soil, allowing more sunlight, heat, and moisture to reach forest floors. It promotes the growth of saplings and shrubs, and helps clear away tangled branches, deadfall, and needles that prevent new plants from growing. Fire also removes insect pests and disease. A very hot fire provides tree roots with more room to seek nutrients and support in the soil.

Natural Resources

The Canadian Shield contains a wealth of natural resources, including minerals, trees, and water. Mining, hydroelectricity, and forestry are the main industries in the Canadian Shield region.

Richness Beneath the Earth

Builders of the Canadian Pacific Railway were among the first to discover the valuable minerals hidden in the Canadian Shield. The minerals include large deposits of gold, silver, nickel, and copper. Iron and zinc can also be found in the region. Mining towns throughout northern Canada extract these mineral resources from the region. Sudbury, Ontario, is one of the largest sources of nickel in the world. It is also one of the leading producers of copper in Canada.

> "Builders of the Canadian Pacific Railway were among the first to discover the valuable minerals hidden in the Canadian Shield."

Minerals taken from the Canadian Shield are used in many ways. For example, Canada is one of the world's leading producers of gold. Almost 85 percent of gold is used for jewellery, coins, and other types of ornaments. Gold is also used in electronics, dentistry, and in the aerospace industry. Nickel has traditionally been used to make coins.

In Canada, the dime and quarter were traditionally made of pure nickel. Today, the dime, quarter, and nickel are made by plating nickel onto steel. More than 60 percent of primary nickel production is used to make stainless steel. More than half of the refined copper in Canada is used for electrical purposes, such as wire.

Iron ore deposits, such as silver, lead, and zinc, have been found in parts of the northern tip of the Canadian Shield.

Energy from Water

The Canadian Shield contains a significant amount of Canada's water. The region has a tremendous capacity to produce hydroelectricity because of its many lakes and rivers. Hydroelectric facilities have been built throughout the Canadian Shield from Newfoundland to Saskatchewan to the Northwest Territories.

Quebec, which is Canada's biggest producer of hydroelectricity, has large hydroelectric facilities. Quebec and Manitoba produce a surplus of electricity, which is sold to the United States. Most hydroelectric power produced in Newfoundland is also sold to the United States.

The Canadian Shield is well-known for its forest industry. Forestry occurs primarily in the boreal forests of Quebec and Ontario.

Forestry

Softwood trees grow in the forests in the southern part of the Canadian Shield. They provide most of the wood for Canada's pulp and paper industry.

ARE THERE DIAMONDS IN CANADA?

Geologists have known for at least 30 years that the Canadian Shield had the right conditions for diamonds to form. However, diamonds have only recently been discovered in this region. Since the late 1980s, intense exploration for diamonds has taken place throughout Canada. Diamonds have been discovered in the part of the Canadian Shield that lies in the Northwest Territories. Diamonds have been discovered in kimberlite pipes. Kimberlite is a type of rock formation found near diamonds. One theory suggests that at, one time, the Canadian Shield was located above a hot spot close to Earth's surface. As the continent drifted over this spot, kimberlite pipes formed in some areas. Diamond-bearing kimberlite has been found north of Yellowknife in the Northwest Territories, as well as in Alberta, Saskatchewan, Manitoba, Ontario, and Quebec.

Soil of the Canadian Shield

Except for a few small areas, the Canadian Shield is generally too rocky to support agriculture. Factors that play a role in the region's poor soil quality are its arctic to subarctic climate, hilly terrain, and acidic vegetation. Where soils occur, they are of variable depth and often coarse-textured.

How Soil Forms

Water and wind help create soil. Wind carries soil from one area to another, while flowing water places sediment in soil. Forest fires can benefit soil growth, but they can also hinder it. Fire can help the soil by quickly releasing nutrients trapped in vegetation. Fire can also destroy soil by burning it.

In the Northern Hemisphere, the most powerful force that shaped soil is glacial ice. In some areas, glacial ice deposited large amounts of soil. In other areas, the soil was completely stripped away.

The Canadian Shield has long stretches of sand and bare rock. A mixture of clay, sand, and humus make up the soil. These elements lack nutrients, causing the soil to be thin, cold, coarse, acidic, and soggy.

Climate conditions in the boreal and taiga forests result in out-growing stands of stunted coniferous trees, such as black spruce and balsam fir. The needles of these trees contain acid, so when the needles fall and decompose, they ooze acid into the soil. This acid reduces the extent of productive forest land.

The greatest production of potatoes on the Canadian Shield is in Manitoba. Potatoes are the most valuable vegetable crop in Canada.

Soil on the Canadian Shield belongs to a group of moderately weathered soils that are common in high-latitude forests. The two main types of soil found in the region are cryosols and brunisols. On the Canadian Shield, cryosols are most often found in muskeg areas, where little heat accesses the ground. Brunisols go through cycles of freezing and thawing. The family of brunisolic and podzolic soils are commonly found in upland sites. The region also contains spodosols, which form on sandy materials under coniferous, mixed coniferous, and deciduous trees.

Permafrost

The extent of permafrost in the ground is variable throughout the Canadian Shield. It is widespread in some spots and scanty in others. Between 30 to 80 percent of the ground in the Canadian Shield has permafrost. Permafrost is ground that remains frozen for at least 2 years. In the Shield, this frozen ground prevents the soil from draining, causing areas near lakes and rivers to be soaked in water. Permafrost is also affected by seasonal changes, causing physical weathering of the bedrock and reducing mudstones to **silts**.

The lowlands of the Canadian Shield, near the Hudson Bay, have soggy soil. Trees grow well in these conditions.

QUICK FACTS

▷ Poor soil means Canadian farmers must rely heavily on science and technology to grow crops. Canadian farming methods are among the most advanced in the world.

▷ Crops that prefer acidic soil, such as potatoes, can be grown in soil that contains spodosols. The soil contains aluminum, iron, and organic matter.

Sparse Plant Life

The Canadian Shield's thin, acidic, soggy soil means that delicate plants cannot survive. Hardy plants have special adaptations to help them live in the region.

When the glaciers first melted, the first plants to appear on the Canadian Shield were probably lichen. Lichens are plants made of fungus and algae. They are often green, grey, or yellowish and appear on rocks and tree trunks. Lichens often grow where nothing else can survive. By themselves, they cover most of the tundra ground in the Canadian Shield. Lichens do not require soil. Rather, they grow by clinging to objects in their surrounding environment.

> **" When glaciers melted, the first plants to appear on the Canadian Shield were lichen. "**

Trees of the Shield

Coniferous trees grow in the northern part of the Canadian Shield, while broadleaf trees grow in the south. Broadleaf trees are **deciduous** trees that have hard wood. Yellow birch trees and sugar maple trees can also be found in the southern part of the Canadian Shield. Other trees that can be found across the Canadian Shield include white and black spruce, balsam fir, eastern red cedar, and paper and white birch. White spruce grows on well-drained ridges. Willows and alders cover bottom lands along streams. Jack pine thrives in sandy areas.

Lichens are found on the branches of spruce and fir trees common in the subalpine forests of the boreal shield.

Little water movement and low levels of oxygen contribute to the slow decay in bogs, which creates a buildup of peat.

Muskeg and Bogs

Most of Canada's muskeg is on the Canadian Shield within the boreal forest. It thrives in moderately cold climate and on gently rolling hills. Precipitation and sphagnum moss also enable growth of muskeg. Muskeg covers 2,000 kilometres of the Canadian Shield, from the Nottaway and Harricanaw Rivers in Quebec, near James Bay, to Churchill, Manitoba.

Bogs in the Canadian Shield are covered in sphagnum moss. Sphagnum moss makes bog water acidic, so few other plants can survive. Shrubs such as Labrador tea, cranberry, and black spruce are able to survive in the acidic conditions. Peat also thrives in bogs.

QUICK FACTS

- Bogs and other wetlands cover one-fifth of the Canadian Shield.

- Lichens can grow in tropical heat as well as cold climates. In laboratories, lichens have been exposed to temperatures of -273° Celsius for hours and survived.

- Coniferous trees begin **photosynthesis** immediately in spring. They can even begin this process during warm spells in the winter if the sunlight is intense enough.

- With about 1.3 million square kilometres of muskeg, Canada has more than any other country in the world.

Animal Life

The Canadian Shield is home to a variety of birds, animals, insects, reptiles, and amphibians. They range from the tiny black fly to the large black bear.

> 66 In the southern forest of the Shield, 20,000 species of insects thrive. 99

Mammals

Numerous mammals inhabit the enormous land area of the Canadian Shield. Large **herbivores** include the woodland and barren-ground caribou, the white-tailed deer, and moose. Smaller **carnivores** include raccoon, striped skunk, eastern chipmunk, beaver, porcupine, and the Arctic hare. Animals such as the marten, short-tailed weasel, ermine, mink, river otter, coyote, and red fox prey upon these smaller mammals. Larger carnivores that live on the Canadian Shield include the black bear, lynx, bobcat, and wolf.

Birds

Many birds live in the Canadian Shield region. Birds of prey include the boreal owl, great horned owl, bald eagle, and turkey vulture. Songbirds, including the cardinal, wood thrush, and white-throated sparrow, share the region with birds of prey.

Owls do not build their own nests. The great grey owl prefers a northern goshawk nest in a larch swamp.

Fourteen species of turtles are found in Canada. They live near ponds, marshes, rivers, and lakes.

Reptiles and Amphibians

Yellow-spotted salamanders, blue-spotted salamanders, eastern redback salamanders, and eastern newts inhabit moist Canadian Shield areas. The maritime garter snake, eastern garter snake, and redbelly snake can also be found throughout the Canadian Shield.

Insects

In the mixed forest and southern part of the Canadian Shield, 20,000 species of insects thrive. At the tree line, about 10,000 species live. About 1,000 species of insects reside north of the tree line.

Some birds, such as sandpipers and northern horned larks, feed on insects. Their diet may include wasps and beetles. Other insects on the Canadian Shield include mites, moths, butterflies, bees, and wood ants.

Fish

With so much water, many types of fish are found in the Canadian Shield. Predatory fish include the lake sturgeon, brook trout, lake trout, northern pike, largemouth bass, and walleye. Some of the fish that they prey upon are lake whitefish, rainbow smelt, and yellow perch.

QUICK FACTS

- During spring, large flocks of waterbirds nest and breed in the Canadian Shield's wetlands. Some of these birds include the common loon, sandhill crane, and the Canada goose.

- Two types of turtles that can be found in the Canadian Shield are the common snapping turtle and the painted turtle.

- Anadramous fish are those that live in the ocean, but enter fresh waters to spawn. The Atlantic salmon is one such fish that spawns in the Canadian Shield region.

Changes and Challenges

Since its historic formation, the Canadian Shield has undergone many changes. Unfortunately, some changes the region is currently experiencing are threatening the plants and animals that live there, and the environment itself.

Some scientists estimate that up to 40 percent of the Canadian Shield's **habitat** remains intact. Small parts of the region have been heavily altered through converting the land to pasture. The largest impact in recent years has been made by logging and the forestry industry.

The Impact of Logging

More than 50 percent of the Canadian Shield has been logged, and more trees will be cut down in the near future. North of Lake Nipigon, Ontario, a large tract of land remains free of logging and human settlement. There are several smaller undisturbed areas of land throughout Ontario and Quebec, especially the area around Lake Mistassini, Quebec, which is located on the northern edge of the region, near the Arctic. There is little land on the Canadian Shield that has not been altered by human settlement or industries.

Logging of trees not only removes mature trees. Birds and insects also lose their homes. Many forests are left with only aspen and birch trees instead of the conifer trees that originally covered the land.

Clearcutting on steep slopes limits wildlife habitat and biodiversity while causing soil erosion.

Mercury Threatens Life

Another threat to animals, birds, and fish in the region is mercury contamination. Facilities produce mercury for many uses, including paint, temperature and pressure measuring devices, and **pharmaceuticals**. Mercury is a naturally occurring metal. The organic form of mercury, methylmercury, is highly toxic. In the Canadian Shield, when mercury enters water, it becomes a threat to the surrounding environment, animals, and humans.

Mercury-contaminated water decomposes vegetation, depleting oxygen levels in the water. Fish are often exposed to mercury when they eat contaminated organisms, such as plants. Fish exposed to mercury can die. Sometimes, fish that have been exposed to mercury are caught and eaten by humans. To protect people, governments in many countries, including Canada, urge people to limit the amount of fish they eat.

Q Should logging be banned in the Canadian Shield region?

NO	YES
Logging provides jobs for many Canadians. Loggers cut down trees, drivers transport the trees, factories employ people, and thousands of people use the logs in the paper, furniture, and home industries.	Forests provide homes for numerous animals, birds, insects, reptiles, and amphibians. When trees are cut down, their habitats are destroyed.
In some areas, trees are cut down to make room for communities. People should be allowed to choose where they want to live.	Logging is affecting the natural balance in the region. Already, the coniferous forests that used to dominate the region are becoming the minority in some areas.
Canada's forest industry accounts for about 3 percent of the country's economy. It is important that Canada continue exporting lumber products.	Trees are cut down faster than new trees have a chance to grow.

View from Above

There are different ways to view a region. Maps and photos, including those from satellites, help to show the region in different ways.

A map is a diagram that shows an area's surface. Maps can demonstrate many details, such as lakes, rivers, borders, towns, and even roads.

Photos can demonstrate what a region looks like close up. In a photo, specific objects, such as buildings, people, and animals, can be seen.

Satellite photos are pictures taken from space. A satellite thousands of metres in the air can show details as small as a car.

Questions:

What information can be obtained from a photo?

How might a map be useful?

What details are indicated on a satellite photo that cannot be seen on a map?

Satellite Image of Clearwater Lakes, Quebec

Clearwater Lakes

Scientists believe the Clearwater Lakes were formed at the same time by the force of two asteroids. They hit Earth about 290 million years ago. The Clearwater Lakes are located in the Canadian Shield region in northern Quebec. The lakes are named after their very clear water.

What do you notice about this satellite photo compared to a regular photo? What information can you learn from it that you would not learn from a map?

Technology Tools

People have studied geology for hundreds of years. Geologists study the rocks, earth, and surfaces that make up Earth. Even before the science of geology had a name, ancient peoples studied the rocks and minerals around them. They experimented to find out what kind of rocks were used to make weapons, jewellery, and items they needed in daily life. Flint, a type of rock that is easy to shape and sharpen, was used to make spears. Minerals, such as gold and copper, were too soft to use as weapons or tools and were shaped to make beautiful jewellery.

Today, geologists use some tools that have been around for centuries, as well as more modern tools. These tools range from simple pick hammers to sophisticated computer equipment. Geologists use these tools to study the rocks and minerals they find on land. They study geology in other areas, as well. Modern technology and tools help them study geology under the sea, in volcanoes, and even on the Moon.

Careers in Geology

What is a geological information systems (GIS) specialist?

Answer: Geological information systems specialists work with geoscientists to produce accurate maps of the location and relationships between rocks. They use remote sensing information from satellites about landscapes, soil, and vegetation. GIS specialists take the information and assemble it into maps.

Tools of the Trade

Rock hammer or pick:

These special hammers have a flat end that is used to crush larger pieces of rock, and a pointed end, which is used to pick away smaller pieces of rock.

X rays:

X rays help geologists study material in detail. Certain crystals or minerals can be examined very closely by an X ray. Geologists studying ancient fossils or artifacts also use X rays so they can examine delicate objects without damaging them.

Compass:

A compass helps geologists tell which direction they are going. Compasses are very important to geologists, who often work from maps to travel to the areas they are studying.

Seismograph:

A seismograph measures Earth's vibrations. Geologists use seismographs to study the movements of Earth's tectonic plates. Tectonic plates are huge slabs of rock that shift and move beneath Earth's surface. When two or more plates collide, there is an earthquake.

Brushes:

Some of the rocks and materials geologists study are very delicate. Once geologists have uncovered an object in the rock or soil, they use soft brushes to remove dust and debris without causing damage.

Sonar:

Sonar helps geologists map areas that cannot be reached by humans or seen by the human eye. Sonar sends out a beam of sound. Geologists determine what the sonar has hit by the type of vibration that returns. They can map these locations by listening to the sound.

What is a glacial geologist?

Answer: Glacial geologists study the physical properties and movement of glaciers. They collect, analyze, and interpret data to try to answer questions about Earth. Someone who enjoys conducting research, mapping, travelling, and working outdoors might be a good glacial geologist.

Make a Topographic Map

A topographic map is a two-dimensional representation of three-dimensional objects. Topographic maps represent shapes, such as mountains, on Earth. You can create your own topographic map to fully understand how topography works.

Materials

Poster paper

Different coloured markers

A wooden skewer

A large piece of Styrofoam, in a ragged shape

A knife that can cut through Styrofoam

Directions

1. Ask an adult to cut your Styrofoam shape into layers that are 1-centimetre thick.

2. Carefully thread the wooden skewer through the Styrofoam pieces to reform the original shape. The wooden skewer must go through straight from the top to the bottom.

3. Place your Styrofoam shape in the centre of the poster paper. Press firmly so that the wooden skewer leaves a mark on the paper. Carefully remove the pieces from the wooden skewer. Place the bottom layer on the poster paper. Make sure that the hole in the centre of the Styrofoam matches with the mark on the paper made by the wooden skewer. Trace around the piece of Styrofoam. Using a different coloured marker, trace around the next layer of the Styrofoam shape.

4. Repeat this process until you have traced all layers. Make sure to use a different colour for each layer.

5. Label each line on your map in centimetres to represent the shape's height. The bottom layer should be labelled zero.

Navigating Your Neighbourhood

Geologists and other scientists who study the Canadian Shield often work deep in the boreal forest. It is important that they have good mapmaking skills so they do not get lost. Maps help geologists navigate, or find their way. This activity will show you how geologists mark their routes so they can find their way into and out of the boreal forest.

Materials

A map of your neighbourhood   Coloured markers

Directions

1. Choose a destination in your neighbourhood. You might choose your school, the grocery store, or a park.

2. On the map, mark your starting point (your house) and the end point (your destination). Use a marker to trace the route you would walk from your house to the destination.

3. With a friend or adult, walk the route on your map. Bring the map with you. As you walk along the streets, are there shortcuts you can take? Maybe there is a pathway between two houses that does not appear on the map. Use a different coloured marker to make changes to the route on your map.

4. When you reach your destination, compare the routes. Did your route change? What might happen if you took a wrong turn?

Further Research

Books

Find out more about the Canadian Shield.

Berton, Pierre. *Steel Across the Shield*. Toronto, ON: McClelland & Stewart, 1994.

DesRivieres, Dennis, Colin M. Bain, and Robert Harshman. *Experience Canada: A Geography*. Don Mills, ON: Oxford University Press Canada, 2003.

Web Sites

To learn more about the Canadian Shield region, visit:

Canadian Council on Ecological Areas
www.ccea.org/ecozones

To find out about the land, climate, and people in the Canadian Shield region, visit:

get2knowcanada.ca
www.get2knowcanada.ca/region_cs.htm

To learn about the different Canadian Shield regions, visit:

ocanada.ca
www.ocanada.ca/geography/regional.php

Glossary

Algonquian: a linguistic family of certain First Nations groups

Algonquin: a First Nations group

anomaly: a departure from the general characteristics of an area

bedrock: solid rock that forms a foundation under loose rock and soil

bogs: wet, spongy ground

boreal forest: the northernmost and coldest forest in the northern hemisphere

carnivores: meat-eating animals

coniferous: trees that bear cones

deciduous: trees that shed at the end of the growing season

erosion: gradual wearing away of rock and soil by wind and water

fjords: long, narrow, deep inlets of the sea between steep slopes

fossils: the rocklike, preserved remains of a plant or animal

habitat: a place or environment where plants and animals live

herbivores: animals that eat plants

ice age: a period of time when Earth was covered in sheets of ice and snow

igneous: rocks or natural substances that become solid from molten material

metamorphic rocks: rocks formed when an existing rock is changed by heat and/or pressure

minerals: natural substances that are neither plants nor animals

muskeg: swamp or marsh

Norse: the people of Scandinavia

Northwest Passage: an Arctic shipping route linking the Atlantic and Pacific Oceans

pharmaceuticals: chemical substances that are used for medicinal purposes

photosynthesis: the process that plants use to make food from water, carbon dioxide, and sunlight

porous: a material that allows water to pass through it

prokaryotes: organisms, such as bacteria, that do not have a nucleus

relief: the shape of the surface showing the changes in high and low points

silts: fine pieces of sand or rock

tundra: a flat, level, treeless plain

Index